The Girl With No Voice

A true story of child abuse, human trafficking, forced prostitution, and then miraculous freedom by the grace of God

Diane Jackson

Times Up for Trafficking Press

The Girl With No Voice

Author: Diane Jackson
Published by: Times Up For Trafficking Press (TUT Press)
An Imprint of SEGR Publishing LLC
Grapevine TX USA
www.SEGRpublishing.com
Editor: Heidi Clingen

ISBN: **978-1-61920-077-7**

Table of Contents

FOREWORD

When I started my advocacy for survivors, Times Up for Trafficking, I felt compelled to warn the public about the massive toll of selling human beings. I also wanted to help survivors of sex trafficking become authors and speakers to tell their own stories. After Diane and I became acquainted online, I assured her that my publishing colleague and I would be there for her, whenever she was ready.

Diane did the rest. I admire her for keeping alive her dream of becoming an author through countless emotional, physical, and spiritual battles. To tell the story of all that was endured is a process that cannot be rushed. Survivors' stories are tender and raw with regret, pain, and bewilderment. They must feel safe as they navigate this complex maze. They need to know they won't endanger themselves by revealing too much, offending support systems, nor retrigger themselves beyond their ability to heal yet again. The motivation must be a heart to help others heal. Diane has such a heart.

The horrid abuse of minors is pervasiveness globally. Authors like Diane will help raise awareness. Readers will experience her treacherous girlhood journey with no place of safety. But she always knew God was there for her when there was no one. She knew He was her Waymaker when there was no way. We believe that the Lord gave her the wisdom to outwit and the strength to escape those who desired to destroy her body and crush her spirit.

Through God's grace and her grandmother's prayers, Diane persisted in surviving. Now she is thriving! For that, we all can be grateful.

Heidi Clingen
Times Up for Trafficking (TUT) Press

This book is dedicated to all the missing Indigenous women in Montana and the Canadian border who have not been found, often left behind by society and the media. May God comfort their loved ones and provide answers.

Chapter One

Diane Pearl Page and the Basement Apartment

The only picture I have of my mother.

The angel of the Lord encamps
around those who fear him,
and he delivers them. Taste and see that
the Lord is good;
blessed is the one who takes refuge in him.
Fear the Lord, you his holy people, for those who
fear him lack nothing.
--Psalm 34:7-9 :7

My story began in my beautiful hometown, Great Falls, Montana in 1962. I was the third child in my family, out of four in total. Unfortunately, I was born into a very abusive family, my father was an extremely aggressive person. He beat my mother.

My first memory was when I was two. My little sister and I were living in a basement apartment with our mother. She was separated from my father, so my brothers were living with my father. I remember vividly that my mother was in tears frequently. She would often apologize to us. She worked and we went to a babysitter. She cooked us lots of hot dogs. She let us have a tabby cat that slept in the bathtub. At night, we shared a bed all together in an empty bedroom.

One night when my sister and I were sleeping and my mother burst in frantically and exclaimed, "Get up, he's coming!" She sat us in front of the television, which past midnight was off the air back then. My father came into our apartment with his arm cut open. Apparently, he had been in a fight, and he wanted our mother to pay for repairing his injuries. He took one look at us and yelled, "Get your asses to bed!" In the bed, hugging each other tight, we could hear our mother's heart-wrenching screams.

Eventually we moved to an apartment building at 909 3rd Ave North with our father's mother. She was an RN despite her age. Soon our mother left us there. Forever. The last time we saw her was when I was three. My sister and I were standing at the front door while she wept and told us she had to go. She handed us two plastic dolls. We had never had a doll and I remember how the dolls' eyes rolled around.

We never saw our mother again. My brother told me that our father had snuck her back in at night and forced her to sleep nude in between my brothers. When I was older, my brothers told me that our father said he cut our mother up and threw her into Smith River. They said our father had taken them to the place he called the snake hole, to show them where he had thrown her body.

Till this day, searching everywhere, offline, and online, I have never been able to find our mother. I pray she did not die at the hands of our Father, but I knew he was cruel enough to kill her.

My mother's parents came a few months later looking for her. My grandma told them she did not know what happened to her. I was standing next to my grandma. She and my mother's parents looked at me so sadly and smiled at me because I looked so much like her.

Chapter Two

Life without Mama

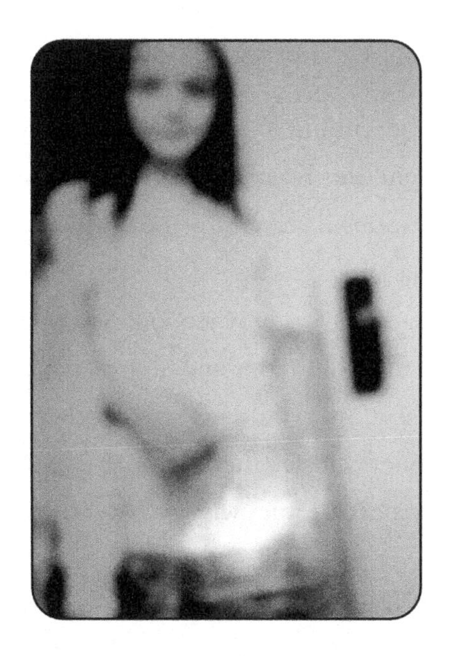

Me at age 9.

But the Lord is faithful,
and he will strengthen you and protect you
from the evil one.
We have confidence in the
Lord that you are doing
and will continue to do the things we command.
May the Lord direct your hearts into God's love
and Christ's perseverance.
--2 Thessalonians 3:3-5

Living without my mother was very hard to endure. Even now, my mind continually questions if she is somehow still alive. My grandma and my father had jobs, so we had a teenage babysitter when our grandma was away. She would taunt and abuse my baby sister and me. She would give my brothers candy and money and let them go out. Meanwhile, she played sick games with us.

When we were hungry, she would prepare food and eat it in front of us as she laughed. Sometimes she forced us into a sleeping bag, zipped it up, and nearly suffocated us. My baby sister screamed as I held her tight. One day we finally told our father what she was doing, and he went looking for her. But he said he never found her.

Dad had a large collection of pornography, which he left around the house. For a while he had a girlfriend. He forced us to line up in a row in front of his bedroom. My brothers were 5 and 4 years old, I was 3, and my baby sister was 1. He made us watch him have sex with his girlfriend. That was bad enough. But then he would make us each come into the room, one at a time, and touch them. It was a tough way to learn about sex. Apparently, our father's girlfriend wasn't happy about it either because she left him. But before she left, she made me brush her hair. I always wondered what that was about. There were so many things that didn't make sense.

Next, we moved to a large house across the street. It belonged to Eddie Myers, who was handicapped, and his mother. They asked us to house sit while they were away. It was large enough for Grandma to have her own master bedroom. All of us kids were kept in the same area, one room for the boys and one room for my sister. I slept in an outer room. I can remember this so vividly because this is where my oldest brother tried to rape me. I cannot speak for my siblings and unfortunately, he committed suicide several years ago.

There were basement apartments in the house, which were rented out. A nice couple lived in one. In the other rented room was a man who would give me candy and take me for rides in his car and sexually mess with me.

He was my father's best friend. I always wondered about that.

Chapter 3

Homeliest Child

My grandmother in her twenties (right) and her husband (left) (1927)

No weapon formed against you will prevail,
and you will refute every tongue that accuses you.
This is the heritage of the servants of the Lord,
and this is their vindication from me,
declares the Lord.
-- Isaiah 54:17

Shortly after this, we moved to 624 Second Ave. South, I started to run away from home. My ability to run fast saved me many times. I could outrun almost anyone. I would only go on short runs like going to Mr. Knudson's house, my grandma's friend. At first, he would give me something to eat. Later on Mr. Knudson started to give me beer, then he would start fondling me. I never told my grandma.

My grandma, Ida Marie Haven, was from Norway. Her parents immigrated to America. They resided in Boston. She had 13 siblings in all! My grandma worked as a Nurse. Later, she married her husband and had one son. Unfortunately, her husband passed away when her son was only 12 years old. She never remarried and gave up her career to help raise us children. She was selfless. She was a godly woman and it showed. She took us to church and worked hard to make our childhood seem "normal." She wasn't around when we were abused, I believe she was fearful of her son. She never beat us or harmed us, that was all her son. I never met many of her family members, my dad-- her son-- didn't like them. She passed away in her 90's and I remember fondly of her wearing a locket, which I gave her. I believe I was kept alive by grandma and her prayers.

One thing I remember most about grandma is that she was very particular about her cleaning.

Since I was the chosen one to help my grandmother with the chores, I did not get to play like my siblings, I never had the privilege of riding a bike or playing with toys. I did not have a typical childhood. All I can remember is cleaning the house. Never was I told "I love you." Instead, every night, my father would squeeze my face as hard as he could and say, "You are the homeliest person ever born! Now, get your ass to bed!"

I knew life would always be like this. Ridiculed every night by my father, forced to clean every day by my grandma. I thought it couldn't get any worse. Then, one day, my life went horribly wrong. My father made me babysit several small children who lived across the street with their mother. One night when I was babysitting, there was a knock at the door. I opened the door to a man who asked to see the mother. I told him she wasn't there.

A few minutes later, he came back, carrying a large cooking pot. How peculiar, I thought. He said he was returning the pot to her, but when I reached for it, he pushed his way into the house. Then he covered my mouth with his hand and forced me into the bedroom where the children were sleeping. He threw me across the bed and started raping me, on top of the children! I screamed for dear life, praying my family across the street would hear me. When he was done with me, he ran out of the house.

The children were sobbing hysterically, so I tried to calm them down. When their mother returned home, I didn't say a word about what happened. I just wanted to get safely to my own home and my own bed. But when I reached my house, the man was standing there, waiting with a friend. He and his friend tried to convince me to leave with them! Fortunately, my father came home, they left, and he told me to get to bed. So, I did.

A few days later, I couldn't stand the pain any longer. I told my grandma my privates were hurting. She looked and could tell what had happened. She told my father I had been raped and she took me to the doctor. I can still feel that cold, metal clamp inside me. The doctor told me that I had an STD.

I was 11 years old.

The police got involved and checked my brothers for infection, to make sure they were not the rapists. My father drove me and one of my brothers around the city until I saw the man working on a car. I yelled, "There he is!" My father pulled over, took a shotgun, and held it on him as my brother and I rushed to call the police. I told my story to a prosecutor, but the rapist was a military man, so the authorities tried to protect him. I had to take a lie detector test, which proved that I was not lying. So, he was charged. The judge told me he deserved to be hung. I don't know how long he served. But I was told that, when his time was up, he was not to be allowed in Montana for twenty-five years.

To this day, I cringe in fear whenever I see the name Robert Coleman.

Chapter 4

The Unwanted Child

Keep me as the apple of your eye; hide me in the shadow of your wings
from the wicked who are out to destroy me, from my mortal enemies who surround me. They close up their callous hearts, and their mouths speak with arrogance.
--Psalm 17:8-10

I kept running away. Just a few days at a time, so they never reported me as a runaway. My father did not miss me. He was happy I was not there. When you never felt love in your childhood, it creates a lifelong loneliness.

My home then was 624 Second Ave. South. In the backyard was a mama cat with her kittens. I would sneak food to her and her kittens. My father must have detected that I cared for them. One day he said, "Cheryl (my childhood name), we are going for a ride". We drove up high in the Cascade Mountains, by some cliffs. He took a box out of the trunk. In it were the baby kittens. He told me to stand near him by a cliff. He took out a pistol and shot each of the kittens and threw them over the cliff. I thought I would be next.

But he took me back to the car and drove to a rocky cove. A rattlesnake was lying there, and he shot it in the head. Next, he took out two shotguns. He told me to sit down, and he showed me how to put the shotgun on my shoulder, squint my eye, and fire. I pulled the trigger, and the gun went off in his direction.

He smacked me full force across the face and told me to never do that again.

I knew in my heart that my father had planned to kill me that day. But God stopped him. He could have just shrugged his shoulders and said, "She ran away again." But after that, I really started to run away. A few people at school tried to help me. But not many options were available to children then. Soon, many people had violated my body.

Eventually I was placed in a juvenile detention center. It felt like a jail. There was no television, but it was by a railroad track, and I would watch the trains pass by. The lady who supervised the detention center was kind to me and told me she did not understand why I was there because I was a good girl.

Chapter 5

Escape to the Natives

So do not fear, for I am with you; do not be
dismayed, for I am your God.
I will strengthen you and help you; I will uphold
you with my righteous right hand.
All who rage against you will surely
be ashamed and disgraced;
those who oppose you will be as
nothing and perish.
Though you search for your enemies,
you will not find them.
Those who wage war against you will be
as nothing at all.
-- Isaiah 41:10-12

No matter what, I kept running away. Eventually I was sent to a group home for troubled youth in Helena, Montana. One cottage was for girls and the other cottage was for boys. Each cottage had house parents. During the week, the house parents were a married couple with a child. On the weekends, we had a house mother who lived downstairs in an apartment. We loved her. But the man who was there during the week liked to play mind games with us. He once paid me five dollars to burn myself with a cigarette. Another time he asked me to show him and the others how to gut a fish. He was very strange and frightening.

One night we snuck out with some of the boys and went to the mountains near a herd of buffalo. I wandered away from the group, for I was a wanderer. Suddenly, a Native American man appeared and tried to convince me to go with him. I ran as fast as I could to the group and told them what happened. We went searching for the man, but eventually returned to our cottages, where the house parents were waiting for us. We were made to scrub the floors with a toothbrush.

The man who ran the house said Native Americans were ugly. I have always been friends with Native Americans. My best friend Ruthie was half Native American. We have been friends since the age of three. We were blood sisters because we cut our fingers and rubbed them together. So she is in my blood.

A girl named Donna lived in our cottage. She had long beautiful hair and was very quiet, yet so full of wisdom. She introduced me to her cousin. He was nineteen, just discharged from the Army. I was about thirteen. Robert was handsome and charming. He started to buy gifts for me. I was so in love with him that I tattooed his initials on my left hand. I still have the tattoo today, for he was my first true love. Soon he talked me into running away with him to the Blackfeet Native reservation. He made me feel beautiful and convinced me that he really loved me, too. He drove up to the girl's cottage one night and I ran away with him.

We lived with his grandmother and his aunt and then we moved into a trailer. There was so much partying and drinking that I told him to go look for work. I believe he would have done anything for me. But soon his grandmother said it was time for me to go and she had the tribal council remove me from the reservation. I returned to Great Falls, and I never saw him again, but I am certain he looked for me. I wished I was older, and I could have stayed with him. But it was not a healthy relationship.

CHAPTER 6

Entrapment

You are my hiding place; you will protect me
from trouble and surround me
with songs of deliverance.
--Psalm 32:7

Back home, I really was not wanted. My brothers drove me to Great Falls High School and dropped me off. I had to ride in the back of the truck in the snow. I walked into the school and looked around the large foyer. Then I turned around and walked out. I couldn't go home, so I spent the day wandering around downtown, cold, and hungry. I wish now that I had snuck back home and hidden in the basement, as I had many times.

Eventually, a girl approached me. She said her name was Vicki. She was about 16 with bleached blonde hair. She asked me if I was alright, and I told her I was scared to go home. She told me I could go home with her where she stayed in a basement room. She snuck me in and got me some food.

I didn't realize it, but Vickie started to groom me. She gave me some clothes. They were seductive. She showed me how to apply makeup. The makeup made me look older. She gave me alcohol, cigarettes, and weed. I wanted to be grown up, and no longer be a vulnerable child, so I tried everything she suggested. Then she said let's go party! For once, I felt pretty. For once I had a friend who cared about me.

Something happened on the way to the party. I ran into my childhood best friend

Ruthie. She is my blood sister, and I know her fighting spirit is still in me. Ruthie pulled me aside and told me to get away from Vicki. How I wish I had listened to her! I miss her and wonder what happened to her. But Vicki interrupted and convinced me that we should run away together. She brought me to a small pickup truck with a shell camper. She put several suitcases in the camper and told me to get in and wait for her. She returned with three white businessmen. She told me they would take care of me. I was scared but I sat quietly as we drove away. That was the last time I saw Montana.

At 13 years old, my first trafficker was another teenage girl.

Chapter 7

Forced to Comply

The Lord is good, a refuge in times of trouble. He cares for those who trust in him.
-- Nahum 1:7

The men drove nonstop through the night. I sat in the back of the truck, frightened and freezing. When they finally stopped, they told me to stay quiet. We were at the Canadian border. I heard footsteps and a border patrol officer and one of the men came to the back of the truck. The man put his wedding ring on my finger in front of the border agent. Nothing more needed to be said and we crossed the border. We drove all the way through Canada to Anchorage, Alaska. There I lived with the three men. They were all married and had money. Two of them took turns abusing me, but one man didn't. He said he had a daughter my age. I had no way to escape or even to use a phone. I stayed inside, cleaning, cooking, and servicing the two men.

But one day I was able to get out of the apartment. I had some coins, I ran to payphone, and I called home. My father answered the phone. I told him I was taken to Alaska by some men, and I wanted to come home. He told me no, there was no room for me. I told him I would sleep on the couch. He said no. I told him I would sleep on the floor. He told me; Cheryl don't come back.

So, I wandered around downtown Anchorage. Again, I was cold and hungry. A lady came out of a business and asked me if I wanted a job, and she would train me. I said yes! Her business was a massage parlor. She gave me one hundred dollars and told me to go buy some sexy clothes. I bought a long dress, but she rejected it; she wanted me to buy lingerie. She kept me in a room and sent men to me. Fortunately, her son took an interest in me and wanted me for himself. That is how I escaped. He let me walk down the stairs by myself. As soon as I reached the door, I ran as fast as I could down the street. He couldn't catch me.

I was still cold and hungry. A man approached me and asked if I needed a place to stay. He took me to a trailer outside of town. I knew I was in trouble when he left to go buy some food for me. I tried to go out the door, but it was locked from the outside. Something told me not to stay there. So I managed to get out through a window. I found the highway and hitchhiked back to town. I went into a bar. But the man was sitting there! So again, I ran away as fast as I could.

Soon I met two men who convinced me they would take me to buy some food. Instead, they took me to a hotel. They stripped me and raped me and filmed me. I was bleeding badly. Finally, they walked out, but they left me two hundred dollars. At last, I could buy some food.

Things were starting to get better. I got something to eat, and I met a nice guy who let me stay in his hotel room. He never touched me. But soon his brother came to the room. He took what was left of my money and slammed my head into a wall. The nice brother intervened, so I grabbed some of my money and ran once again.

I went to a Holiday Inn to buy a hot meal and get a drink. When I was served liquor, I realized it was a set up. I was arrested for solicitation.

No one seemed to care that I was 13 and homeless.

Yet another man bailed me out of jail. He took me on an airplane. He ordered liquor for us. The stewardess never even questioned it. We landed in Louisiana. The man told me to lay out in the sun for a few days so I wouldn't look so pale, then he took me to Dallas, Texas and left me in a cheap motel room. He gave me a phone number to call. Life was moving pretty fast.

Chapter 8
Coming to Texas

When you pass through the waters, I will be with you; and when you pass through the rivers, they will not sweep over you. When you walk through the fire, you will not be burned; the flames will not set you ablaze.

-- Isaiah 43:2

The man who brought me to Texas sent one of his girls to pick me up. She brought me to some studio apartments. There I was introduced to my new pimp. She took me to an upstairs room and told me you will sleep in here. He came in the room and handed me two black pills and said take these. Later I learned they were called black males and he kept all his girls on a steady diet of them. Then he gave me the rules: Tell the police that you are 18. Don't kiss your "dates." And most of all, don't ever look at another pimp. These were the rules I would have to live by. Or nearly die by violating them.

He told me to clean up, get dressed, and go to a club with his "top" girl. The club was on 2nd Avenue in Dallas called the Hawaiian Lounge. It had a motel next to it. I remember walking into a club for the first time. My new pimp was sitting at the bar. He looked me up and down and bragged to other pimps about his recent "purchase," like I was a piece of meat.

I was about to turn fourteen.

He had me sit in a booth. There were pool tables in the back of the club and a steady flow of men. They would buy drinks for the girls and choose which one they wanted. Then the pimp would make them get a room at the motel. A man took me to a room at the hotel. I only remember the first man and how scared I was. I looked up at the ceiling and blanked out.

I learned to space out at a young age; it is a survival mode. It's amazing what the mind can do to help you get through things.

My ability to dissociate was crucial to my survival. Eventually the pimp noticed that I was frequently requested. That helped because the pimp put me into my own studio apartment. The front door was always watched, so I could not escape. But at least I could be alone occasionally. And soon the pimp started to trust me. He let me drive his Cadillac and pick up another girl who was my age. He called us his tribe. I knew better than to think this was a good place for me to be. But at least I felt safer than being out on the streets.

Eventually, that changed.

I didn't know about the gorilla part of the pimp. But I soon learned the hard way. After a long day of seeing the men, I returned to my apartment. He was standing on the stairwell above me. He ran down the stairs, pulled out a pistol, and started to whip me with it. Why? Because a new girl in our tribe had told him I would not talk to her. It didn't matter if that was true or not. She knew how to climb to the top, and I was in her way. A friendly tribe we were not.

The next time took everything I had and has never left me. On a hot summer day, I was being purchased by a group of men. I was sent to see one at a time. The other girls were mad because they hadn't been picked. Maybe I felt a bit proud of myself somehow, in a twisted sort of way. Proverbs 16:18 says pride comes before the fall. But for whatever reason, I slipped up and broke the cardinal rule of pimps.

When I walked back into the club, another pimp smiled at me. It was so nice to be smiled at that I smiled back. Without thinking. That is how easy it can happen. That was a nearly fatal mistake. But God saved me.

In the rules of the street, if you are a top earner and you look at another pimp, you now belong to the new pimp. My pimp had told me the rule to not look at another pimp. I just didn't take it seriously enough, but I would pay for that smile. Later that evening, my pimp brought out his gorilla side again. He burst into my room, forced me to strip naked and lie down on the bed with my soles together and my arms behind my head. Then he began to explain the rule I had broken. He gathered thick metal hangers, untied them, and then twisted them together. Then he said don't you ever look at another pimp, or I will kill you!

He started to whip me with the twisted hangers. All over my body. I blanked out, but it felt like it went on forever. Once he got started, he couldn't seem to stop. He knew he was messing me up for life. That is what he wanted, even though I was his highest earner. I still suffer every day from seeing the scars. I still suffer every day from the nerve damage. For that one smile, he scarred me permanently, emotionally, and physically.

Somehow, I was able to keep on working. I was too terrified to say no to him. And thanks be to the Lord, I didn't lose my mind or try to take my life. Or his. And eventually, a path out appeared. A Latin man came into the club. He pretended to be a client, but he spoke to me in secret about getting me out of there. A few days later he came in again. This time he whispered, "In about ten minutes, sneak out of the club, dash across the street to the furniture store." Across the street, I found him waiting in a car. He drove me into an apartment that was next door to where he lived. He told me to wait there.

Soon, I heard my pimp yelling, "Where is she? I am going to kill her!" The Latin man knew it was too dangerous for me to stay there, so in the dark of night, he moved me out into the rural area of town. He left me with migrant workers. Soon he brought two more girls from my original pimp. He really raided the tribe. He brought a newer girl and the one who said I didn't speak to her and yes, I was back with migrant workers.

Even this didn't last long. Soon the Latin man loaded us up and brought us to Homestead, Florida. I was being treated like chattel. But at least I was alive.

CHAPTER 9
Taken from Texas

But you, O LORD, are a shield about me, my glory, and the lifter of my head.
-- Psalm 3:3

In Homestead, Florida, my new pimp rented a room. He and his buddy kept the other girls in the room and made me go and work on the highway corridor. But a short time later, they left town and left me behind. I had made them enough money to move on. Once again, I was on my own. But I was only fourteen years old. I didn't have a fake ID to rent a room. Nor did I have any money. Once again, I was fighting to survive. So, I went to the highway and stuck out my thumb, hoping I could hitchhike my way to safety.

A deputy sheriff pulled over and asked me what I was doing. I told him I had been abducted. He told me to get into the car. I thought, "He's going to help me!" He brought me to his house and said you can stay here. I cooked and cleaned for him. Unfortunately, he sexually abused me and burned me with cigarettes. When he left for work, he told me I was being watched. A neighbor lady saw me and asked me who I was. I said nothing, so she asked him, and he told her I was his daughter visiting.

Apparently, he didn't want to take any more risks. Shortly later, he took me back to the highway where he had picked me up. He said, "Get out and keep your mouth shut!" I learned that even people wearing a uniform are not always nice people.

So once again, I was wondering how to survive. When I was sitting on a bench, a truck with a family of Puerto Ricans pulled up and asked me if I wanted to go to work picking oranges. I would make five dollars for every bushel I picked. That sounded better than nothing, so I went with them. They took me to an old house with no running water. I could hear rats scampering in the walls. I had to sleep with their oldest son. I would cry every time he crawled on top of me.

We worked six days a week. They kept my money in exchange for food and a place to sleep. And, of course, on Sunday, they would sell me to other workers. One son spoke English and his mother tried to keep me away from him. But one time he and I had to go to the cemetery next to the house to wash off with a water hose. I kept begging him to please help me to escape. Finally, he agreed.

One night he said let's go and we took off running. He had called a friend in Alabama who lived in the mountains, and he told him he could take me there. I remember hiding in ditches with him as his brother was searching for us. Then we got a Greyhound bus ride to Alabama. There was no way I could have done it without him.

He actually cared for me and walked away from his family to help me. There were so few people who really did care.

CHAPTER 10

Escaping Florida, Into the Fire of Alabama

Be strong and courageous. Do not be afraid or terrified because of them,
for the LORD your God goes with you; he will never leave you nor forsake you.
-- Deuteronomy 31:6

After the boy and I arrived in Alabama, we walked up a country road in the cold mountains. Fortunately, we found a deserted house and built a fire and fell asleep. Suddenly we woke up, smelled smoke, and saw that the fire had burned a huge hole in the floor. So, we continued trudging up the mountain. We finally found his friend's house. He and his girlfriend were nice to us and fed us. We stayed there through winter.

But once again I felt trapped. I just wanted to be free. When spring came, I decided it was time to leave, so I began walking down the mountain. The boy followed me, crying. I told him to leave me. The last I saw of him, he was still crying, but in the back of a police car driving away. I hope he found his family.

Once again, I had to figure out how to survive. I was fifteen years old, in a new state, and moving from one trauma to the next. People passed me by like used goods. If they paid any attention to me, it was just to trap me in their games.

Eventually I was discovered by another pimp. It seemed to be the only way I could get food to eat and a place to stay. This one locked me in a hotel room and sent men to my room. The hotel had several floors. I was allowed to go down to the vending machine to get something to eat, but the elevator man always watched me. Once I was commanded to go to another man's room. But I refused because he had a doctor's bag, and I knew he was evil. Finally, the man paid the pimp so much that they forced me to go with him. In his room, he inserted hooks in me, pulling me apart, then he shoved his fist up in me. I blacked out because of the pain.

I knew I had to escape this place too, so when I was allowed to go down the elevator to get something to eat, I ran out as fast as I could. Running was a way of life for me.

No surprise, but I ran into the arms of another pimp. He took me to his house and kept me in his basement apartment where he kept a "stable" of women. I was the new girl, the very bottom rank. He saw my injuries from the man with the doctor's bag and he made me soak for long hours in a bathtub.

Finally, he decided I was ready to work again. He took me to a high-class hotel with some other girls. But I was ready to run again. I met a man who didn't want to use me. He actually helped me. He brought me to a lady who took me in, in exchange for babysitting her son. I had my own room. I felt safe. But soon that changed when the lady got a new boyfriend. The boyfriend kicked me out of her house, back on the street. I will always remember that her son was crying because he wanted me to stay. At least someone wanted me.

Then I met a young pimp. He housed me in another low-down hotel and made me walk the street. That is when I had another close call with death. But God saved me once again. A white man in a white van picked me up. Instead of taking me to his home or a hotel room, he drove me deep into the woods. I somehow sensed he was going to try to kill me. I had mace in my bag, and I tried to reach for it. But he noticed, pulled the car to the side of the road, and raped me horribly. Somehow, I knew that I had to lie still, to not cry out or fight him. I believe that is why I made it out alive. Maybe someone fearless was not attractive to his sick mind. I was so grateful when he took me back to where he found me. When the young pimp found me there, he beat me for being gone too long. At least he didn't kill me.

This was a dangerous place to be. Another day, an old white man picked me up and drove me out to a ravine. He made me to remove clothes and perform a sex act on him in the car. Then he said, I am going to kill you. He started laughing hysterically, nonstop, and I believed him. I knew I needed God to save me yet again. I got the idea to say that I had to pee. Miraculously, the man let me get out to go to the back of the car to pee. That was the first miracle. When I reached the back of the car, he spun the tires, spewing gravel all over me. He was still howling with laughter. But by the grace of God, I saw a way out. I was naked and barefoot, but I decided to run up the ravine anyway. He could not catch me, because he had to drive out. I somehow reached the highway. That was the second miracle. I stuck out my thumb. At that point, I didn't care who picked me up. And I don't even remember who did. But whoever did, they gave me a coat to cover up. And they didn't kill me. That was a miracle, too.

Somehow, I was always able to survive by running away or by talking my way out. I can't count how many men I have survived from murdering me. I just have to note that the majority of these men were white middle-aged men.

Chapter 11

Finally Free

Me at age 17, finally free in Dallas, TX.

The righteous person may have many troubles,
but the LORD delivers him from them all.
-- Psalm 34:19

I ran into another pimp who was actually kind to me. He had an injured eye. He would monitor my dates, he never left me alone. He once gave me a necklace, which I still have. I think he fell in love with me. Soon, he brought me back to Dallas, back where I started two and a half years before. We were in East Dallas on Live Oak Street by Carroll and by Gaston Avenue. His friend who was also a pimp had an apartment. He also had a young white girl, around fourteen. He too, started to have feelings for me. This was the beginning of the Lord turning things around for me. The two pimps put money in a coat and told me I could leave. That is why I remember them the most. They never hurt me, and they helped me escape. I know that God placed me back in Texas for a reason.

This is the end of my trafficking story, just the highlights of all the evil God has delivered me from. Only by the grace of God I was able to endure this.

I have been silent for many years and for many reasons. One reason is the way people look at you when you tell them that you were sex trafficked as a child. Since I have recently started to tell my story, people have told me I am a liar, a whore, and a lunatic. But my Father in Heaven Abba knows that I am telling the truth.

All I want to do is tell how much evil I survived and how I survived it. I knew that from the day of my birth, Satan had tried to kill me. But I know that God chose me from my mother's womb, and He protected me all the way.

There were many men who tried to kill me, but the first man was my father. He denied me as his own and said he cut up my mother into pieces and threw her in the Smith River. I don't have any reason to doubt him. I still miss her so much and I have searched for her all these years. I guess my mother is gone.

But I am still alive. I can still make a difference in this world.

Chapter 12

New Beginnings

There is no fear in love. But perfect love drives out fear, because fear has to do with punishment. The one who fears is not made perfect in love.
-- 1 John 4:18

My first husband did help me escape, but we didn't stay together long. I worked at Sonic and a Mexican restaurant to get back on my feet. Then, I met my children's father and had two daughters with him. With him, I faced brutal abuse, but I thought that was normal. That felt like all I deserved, what I was conditioned into feeling my whole life, so I stayed with him.

Finally, I had to raise my children alone. I worked as much as I could, and we went to church three times a week. I worked hard to get my GED and my CNA license, Certified Nurse's Aide license. I wish I could have gone further with my Nursing career, but I never felt worthy. I was always made to feel like I had to keep quiet about my hardships. Now, I realize that I do deserve good things from God. I did not repeat the abuse and beatings that I endured as a child. I wanted my daughters to have a better life. I wanted them to become Christ followers. How I did it, I will never know. But I do know that If it wasn't for God, we would not have made it through. And many thanks belong to my prayer warrior Grandmother. Without her prayers, I would have been lost forever.

The social workers I shared my story with were astonished at all the brutality I endured.

I thank the Lord that my daughters turned out to be independent, loving, kind, and hard-working. My daughter, Amie works so hard and is truly amazing. She has a beautiful and talented daughter, Chastity, also works hard and is so wonderful at her career. My youngest daughter, Diana, is also a hard worker. She has a beautiful daughter, Melanie, and a handsome son, Andrew.

I love my grandchildren so much. They all turned out to be such wonderful people and always answer my calls and help me whenever I need them. Andrew is so intelligent and is always sweet and loving. I'd like to give special recognition to my granddaughter, Melanie, for helping me to produce this book. She always goes the extra mile for me. I am so happy that she is going down the path of advocating for the oppressed. All Glory is to God for blessing me with the best children and grandchildren in the world.

I need to mention that this book has only a few photos. The first reason is that my childhood was not loving. I was not cherished as other children are. The second reason is that when I was taken from Montana, all my childhood photos were left behind. I have photos of my family, but do not want to include them, to protect their privacy.

I wrote this book for those who are going through their own struggles with healing from childhood abuse or sex trafficking. I want them to know that, even if people don't know your story or don't care about your story, keep telling it. I hope that throughout whatever you have had to endure, you will never lose your faith in the Lord. He loves you and He can see you through. Thank you to Jesus for walking me through all this evil to the other side, where I can now try to help others

Out of my distress I called on the Lord; the Lord answered me and set me free.

-- Psalm 118:5

I wrote this little poem for all the little girls
out there who feel alone.

The Girl Nobody Loved

My journey was so long,
Whoever cared for me?
What was my life about?

Don't call me weak.
I fought for justice.
But no one listened.

I wish everyone had a soul,
But they crave fame and fortune,
And money is their only love.

I'm sorry if I disappointed you.
I should feel shame.
But all I've ever felt was pain.

For Anyone Who is in Human Trafficking or Who Wants to Run Away

Q: What are some warning signs of human trafficking?

A: The warning signs may be hard to detect. Children can be carefully groomed and lured through relationships. Often the new friend is online. Traffickers try to lure children by pretending to be another child online. Therefore, parents must insist on monitoring their children's online activities. Then traffickers often offer to buy presents such as candy, makeup, and clothes. Watch for new possessions that your child can not explain.

In person, your child could be lured and groomed by other children at school. The children may be working alone, or they may be coached by other adults. It is sad to say, but these days you need to be watchful of other parents. So many people have discovered that sex trafficking of children is extremely lucrative. Children should never go to someone's house that they don't know. Meet the parents first. Tell your children that if they feel uncomfortable around other children or adults for any reason, they should tell you.

Q: How can we help victims and survivors of human trafficking?

A: Never judge or blame a victim/survivor. Never ask them, "Why didn't you leave? Why didn't you run away?" They may not have had an opportunity to leave, or they may have been too afraid. Maybe they didn't feel they had any options. I left often, but that didn't solve my problems.

Listen to the survivors; don't speak over them. If someone confides in you, listen and believe! It's your duty as a human being to believe and to find help as soon as possible.

Survivors need places that are safe and caring. Ongoing therapy, housing, and support are needed in the healing process. Don't expect survivors and victims to transition back into regular life quickly. It takes time to heal.

We also need to make sure we are continuously praying for them and their guidance. Include their safety in your prayers to God. The Lord is what kept me safe during this time, I believe my grandmother's prayers were a big part of my survival.

Q: What should someone do if they are considering running away?

A: Anyone who wants to run away from home should reach out to a trusted adult such as a relative, a school counselor, or someone at a church. They can call the runaway hotline (1-800-786-2929). My advice, that I learned the hard way, is don't run away. Especially do not run to a stranger. They can manipulate and take advantage of you, as so often happened to me.

Many runaways are sold into human trafficking. So please, don't run away.

If you're being emotionally or sexually abused, find a safe haven. Go to a church, a community center, or a shelter. Look for places marked as "A Safe Place," such as some gas stations. There you can ask for help and they will contact the authorities for you.

Another key thing is to turn to God for His wisdom and guidance. Spend some time in prayer and meditate upon it. Journal your thoughts and speak it to a friend and/or God.

Q: What are some resources for those trapped in human trafficking?

A: You can call the Human Trafficking Hotline, (888-373-7888). They also can be reached by texting the word HELP to BEFREE (233733). Flyers with this information can be place in restrooms, hotels, and public places with suspected human trafficking.

If you see someone who you think might be trafficked, do not approach them or their captor or "pimp." That could be dangerous. Instead, call the Human Trafficking Hotline for help.

Q: What is your advice to teens, in general?

A: If you're having family issues, such as divorce or abuse, reach out to a friend, trusted adult, police, social worker, or a counselor. Even if you are being threatened, TELL someone. Talk until someone listens. If you're scared to go home, sit in the school office, and refuse to go home. It can feel like everyone in the world is against you but know that God is always for you. No matter what mistakes you make and what path you're currently on, He will always listen and help you. There are people that want to be there for you, it just may take a little more time to find them. But please know that God and Jesus Christ are always there to listen.

Q: How can one cope with the mental trauma inflicted upon them in human trafficking?

A: Talk about it, even though it hurts. I reached out to those that are trapped in human trafficking. I helped them, and that really helped me. But you must heal yourself first before trying to help others.

Therapy and speaking to professionals about your trauma are very important to healing. Don't expect your trauma to disappear quickly; it takes time to heal. It took too long for people to listen to me and believe me about the horrors I went through as a child. But when people started to listen and believe, I started to heal. Another important thing is seeking God for restoration, through prayer for guidance of healing. Finding Christ Jesus will help you more than any human can. Turn it all over to Him. But there's also no shame in speaking to a professional. You could even seek out a therapist who includes God within meetings.

Thank you for reading my story and
for believing.
This has helped me heal even more.
I am praying for everyone out there who
needs to heal, too.
God bless you.
- Diane

Acknowledgments

I never thought I would be writing this book. Throughout my life, I've always been told to shut up about my past. If it wasn't for my granddaughter, Melanie, and her encouragement, it would have never even been started. Next, I would like to express my gratitude towards Heidi Clingen, whom I met through Human Trafficking Facebook pages. I felt in my heart that God was telling me that Heidi was going to help me. Heidi has been an inspiration for many survivors and I'm glad God placed her in my life-- she never gave up nor judged. Heidi also introduced me to a kind man, Bob

Bare. Bob has been helping me to achieve my dream-- via his many talents in the book industry. I believe that Heidi and Bob were both led to me by the Lord and have helped me tremendously, from the graciousness of their hearts and their Godly ways.

Made in the USA
Las Vegas, NV
06 November 2021